The Complete Needlepoint Book

A Comprehensive Guide for Newcomers

Imran Z Cuthbert

THIS BOOK
BELONGS TO

....

....

With so many books out there to choose from, I want to thank you for choosing this one and taking precious time out of your life to buy and read my work. Readers like you are the reason I take such passion in creating these books.

It is with gratitude and humility that I express how honored I am to become a part of your life and I hope that you take the same pleasure in reading this book as I did in writing it.

Can I ask one small favour? I ask that you write an honest and open review on Amazon of what you thought of the book. This will help other readers make an informed choice on whether to buy this book.

My sincerest thanks.

Table of Contents

SUMMARY
- CHAPTER ONE ... 27
  - STORAGE BIN ... 27
  - MATERIALS ... 28
  - DIRECTIONS ... 29
  - STITCHING THE BOX ... 34
  - ADDING FABRIC ... 38
  - GATHERING THE BOX ... 40
- CHAPTER TWO ... 46
  - MOD TABLE RUNER ... 46
  - STITCHING THE CIRCLES ... 49
  - JOINING THE CIRCLES ... 57
- CHAPTER THREE ... 67
  - NEEDLEPOINT STITCH MARKER CASE ... 67
  - MATERIALS ... 68
- CHAPTER FOUR ... 86
  - LAZY DAISY EMBROIDERY ... 86
  - SUPPLIES ... 88
  - STAGE 1 - ENTER THE NET. ... 88
  - STAGE 2 – BASE ... 89
  - STAGE 3 - PETAL FIRST ... 90
  - STAGE 4 - SECURE PETAL ... 91
  - STAGE 5 – REPEAT ... 92
  - LAZY DAISY STITCH TIPS ... 94
  - LAZY DAISY STITCH – THE ... 95
  - INCLUSION ... 95
- CHAPTER FIVE ... 95
  - TINY HEARTS WITH SCROLL STITCH ... 95
  - TOOLS / MATERIALS ... 96
  - GUIDELINES ... 97

SUMMARY

What is The Needlepoint: The Needlepoint is a traditional form of embroidery that involves stitching intricate designs onto a canvas using a needle and thread. It is a popular craft that has been practiced for centuries and is often associated with creating decorative pieces such as tapestries, pillows, and wall hangings.

The process of needlepoint involves creating a pattern or design on a canvas that is made up of small squares or holes. The design is then stitched onto the canvas using a variety of different stitches, such as the tent stitch, the basketweave stitch, or the cross stitch. These stitches are carefully placed to create the desired image or pattern.

One of the unique aspects of needlepoint is the wide range of materials that can be used. While traditional needlepoint uses wool or silk threads, modern needlepoint artists often experiment with different types of threads, such as metallic or variegated threads, to add texture and visual interest to their work. Additionally, needlepoint can be done on a variety of different canvases, including cotton, linen, or even plastic.

The Needlepoint is not only a creative outlet but also a therapeutic activity. Many people find the repetitive motion of stitching to be calming and meditative, allowing them to relax and unwind. It can also be a social activity, with needlepoint groups and clubs providing a space for enthusiasts to come together and share their love for the craft.

In recent years, needlepoint has experienced a resurgence in popularity, with more and more people discovering the joy of creating their own unique pieces. There are now countless patterns and designs available, ranging from traditional and classic to modern and abstract.

Additionally, needlepoint kits and supplies can be easily found online or in craft stores, making it accessible to beginners and experienced stitchers alike.

Overall, The Needlepoint is a versatile and timeless craft that allows individuals to express their creativity and create beautiful, one-of-a-kind pieces. Whether you are a beginner or an experienced stitcher, needlepoint offers a rewarding and enjoyable way to relax, create, and connect with others who share a passion for this ancient art form.

Why Needlepoint Is a Timeless Craft: Needlepoint is a craft that has stood the test of time and continues to captivate people of all ages and backgrounds. Its enduring popularity can be attributed to several factors, including its rich history, therapeutic benefits, and the ability to create unique and personalized pieces.

One of the main reasons why needlepoint is considered a timeless craft is its deep-rooted history. Dating back thousands of years, needlepoint has been practiced by various cultures around the world. From ancient Egypt to medieval Europe, needlepoint has been used to create intricate tapestries, clothing embellishments, and decorative items. This long-standing tradition has helped needlepoint maintain its relevance and appeal throughout the ages.

Furthermore, needlepoint offers numerous therapeutic benefits that contribute to its timelessness. Engaging in this craft requires focus, concentration, and attention to detail, which can help individuals relax and unwind. The repetitive nature of stitching can have a calming effect on the mind, making needlepoint an excellent form of stress relief. Additionally, the act of creating something with one's hands can provide a sense of accomplishment and boost self-esteem. These therapeutic qualities make needlepoint a popular choice for individuals seeking a creative outlet or a way to escape the pressures of everyday life.

Another reason why needlepoint remains a timeless craft is its versatility and ability to create unique and personalized pieces. With a wide range of patterns, colors, and stitches to choose from, needlepoint allows individuals to express their creativity and create one-of-a-kind works of art. Whether it's a small ornament, a decorative pillow, or a large tapestry, needlepoint offers endless possibilities for customization. This ability to create personalized pieces ensures that needlepoint will always have a place in the hearts of craft enthusiasts who value individuality and self-expression.

Moreover, needlepoint is a craft that can be enjoyed by people of all ages and skill levels. From beginners to experienced stitchers, anyone can learn and master the art of needlepoint. The simplicity of the basic stitches makes it accessible to beginners, while the more advanced techniques and intricate designs provide a challenge for seasoned stitchers. This inclusivity and adaptability make needlepoint a craft that can be enjoyed by individuals of all backgrounds and abilities, ensuring its continued popularity for generations to come.

In conclusion, needlepoint is a timeless craft that has endured throughout history due to its rich heritage, therapeutic benefits, and the ability to create unique and personalized pieces.

Understanding the Basics of Needlepoint: Needlepoint is a popular form of embroidery that involves stitching decorative designs onto a canvas using a needle and thread. It is a versatile and creative craft that allows individuals to create beautiful and intricate designs on various items such as pillows, wall hangings, and even clothing.

To begin understanding the basics of needlepoint, it is important to familiarize oneself with the necessary materials and tools. The primary material used in needlepoint is the canvas, which is typically made of cotton or linen and comes in various sizes and mesh counts. The mesh count refers to the number of stitches per inch, with higher counts resulting in finer details. Additionally, a needlepoint canvas can be either blank or pre-printed with a design, depending on the individual's preference.

In terms of tools, a needlepoint enthusiast will need a tapestry needle, which has a large eye and a blunt tip to prevent snagging the canvas. The size of the needle will depend on the mesh count of the canvas, with larger needles used for lower mesh counts and smaller needles for higher mesh counts. Other essential tools include embroidery scissors for cutting thread, a needle threader for easier threading, and a hoop or frame to hold the canvas taut while stitching.

Once the materials and tools are gathered, it is time to learn the basic stitches used in needlepoint. The most common stitch is the tent stitch, also known as the continental stitch, which involves bringing the needle up through the canvas and then down again in a diagonal direction. This stitch is repeated in rows or columns to create a solid and even coverage of the design. Another commonly used stitch is the basketweave stitch, which provides a more textured and three-dimensional effect.

In addition to these basic stitches, needlepoint offers a wide range of decorative stitches that can be used to add interest and complexity to a design. These stitches include the French knot, the satin stitch, the cross stitch, and many more. Each stitch has its own unique technique and effect, allowing needlepoint enthusiasts to experiment and create their own personalized designs.

Understanding the basics of needlepoint also involves learning about color and thread selection. Needlepoint threads come in various materials, such as cotton, silk, wool, and metallic, each offering different textures and finishes. It is important to choose threads that complement the design and canvas, considering factors such as color, thickness, and sheen. Additionally, needlepoint designs often require blending different colors and shades to create depth and dimension.

Essential Tools and Supplies of Needlepoint: Needlepoint, a popular form of embroidery, requires a variety of essential tools and supplies to ensure a successful and enjoyable stitching experience. Whether you are a beginner or an experienced needlepointer, having the right tools at your disposal is crucial for achieving beautiful and intricate designs.

One of the most important tools for needlepoint is, of course, the needle itself. Needles specifically designed for needlepoint are typically longer and have a larger eye compared to regular sewing needles. This allows for easier threading of various types of threads and yarns commonly used in needlepoint. Additionally, the length of the needle helps in maneuvering through the canvas and creating precise stitches.

Another essential tool is the embroidery hoop or frame. This device holds the canvas taut, preventing it from puckering or distorting while you stitch. Hoops come in various sizes and materials, such as wood or plastic, allowing you to choose the one that best suits your project's size and your personal preference. Some needlepointers prefer using stretcher bars, which provide a more rigid and even tension across the canvas.

Thread or yarn is a fundamental supply in needlepoint, and there are countless options available. Traditional needlepoint threads include wool, silk, and cotton, each offering its own unique characteristics and textures. Wool threads are commonly used for their warmth and durability, while silk threads provide a luxurious sheen. Cotton threads, on the other hand, offer a wide range of colors and are often used for their affordability. Additionally, specialty threads like metallic or variegated threads can add extra dimension and visual interest to your needlepoint projects.

To transfer your design onto the canvas, you will need a marking tool. Water-soluble fabric markers or pencils are commonly used for this purpose, as they allow for easy removal once the stitching is complete. Alternatively, you can use a lightbox or transfer paper to trace your design onto the canvas.

Scissors are an essential tool for any needlepointer. They are used for cutting threads and yarns, as well as trimming excess fabric. It is important to have a pair of sharp, pointed scissors specifically designated for needlepoint to ensure clean and precise cuts.

Other supplies that come in handy during the needlepoint process include a needle threader, especially useful for those with visual impairments or difficulty threading needles, and a needlepoint stand or lap frame, which provides a comfortable and ergonomic stitching position.

Lastly, a good reference book or pattern is invaluable for inspiration and guidance.

Preparing Your Canvas and Threads of Needlepoint:

Needlepoint is a popular form of embroidery that involves stitching intricate designs onto a canvas using a needle and thread. Before you can begin your needlepoint project, it is important to properly prepare your canvas and select the appropriate threads.

To start, you will need a canvas specifically designed for needlepoint. These canvases are typically made of cotton or linen and come in various sizes and mesh counts. The mesh count refers to the number of stitches per inch, with a higher count indicating a finer canvas. Choose a canvas that suits your desired design and level of detail.

Once you have your canvas, it is important to prepare it before you start stitching. Begin by stretching the canvas to remove any wrinkles or creases. You can do this by tacking the edges of the canvas onto a wooden frame or using a stretcher bar. This will ensure that your stitches are even and the finished piece looks professional.

Next, you will need to secure the edges of the canvas to prevent fraying. You can do this by using masking tape or sewing a fabric binding around the edges. This step is crucial as it will prevent the canvas from unraveling and make it easier to handle while stitching.

Now that your canvas is prepared, it's time to select the threads for your needlepoint project. Needlepoint threads come in a variety of materials, including cotton, silk, wool, and metallic. Each type of thread has its own unique characteristics and is suitable for different types of designs.

When choosing threads, consider the color palette of your design and the desired effect you want to achieve. Cotton threads are commonly used for their durability and wide range of colors. Silk threads, on the other hand, are known for their lustrous sheen and smooth texture. Wool threads are great for creating texture and adding depth to your needlepoint, while metallic threads can add a touch of sparkle and glamour.

It is important to note that needlepoint threads come in different thicknesses, or plys. The most common plys are single, double, and three-ply. Thicker threads are typically used for larger areas of stitching, while thinner threads are ideal for intricate details.

Before you start stitching, it is a good idea to create a thread inventory. This involves organizing and labeling your threads according to color and type. This will make it easier to find the right thread when you need it and prevent any confusion or mistakes during the stitching process.

Reading Needlepoint Patterns of Needlepoint: When it comes to the art of needlepoint, one of the most important skills to master is the ability to read needlepoint patterns. These patterns serve as a guide for creating intricate and beautiful designs on a canvas using a needle and thread. Understanding how to interpret and follow these patterns is essential for any needlepoint enthusiast.

Needlepoint patterns are typically presented in the form of a chart or graph, which consists of a grid made up of squares. Each square represents a single stitch, and the colors or symbols within the squares indicate the type of stitch to be used and the color of thread to be used. The chart also includes a key that provides a legend for the symbols or colors used in the pattern.

To read a needlepoint pattern, it is important to start by familiarizing yourself with the key. This will help you understand the symbols or colors used in the chart and their corresponding stitches. Once you have a clear understanding of the key, you can begin to interpret the pattern.

The first step in interpreting a needlepoint pattern is to identify the starting point. This is usually indicated by a bold line or arrow on the chart. It is important to begin stitching from this point to ensure that the design is centered and symmetrical.

Next, you will need to determine the direction in which to stitch. This is typically indicated by arrows or lines on the chart. Following these directions will ensure that your stitches are consistent and flow smoothly throughout the design.

As you work through the pattern, it is important to pay attention to any special instructions or symbols that may be included. These instructions may indicate a specific stitch technique to be used or a color change within the design. Following these instructions will help you achieve the desired result and bring the pattern to life.

Reading needlepoint patterns also requires attention to detail. It is important to count the number of squares in each row and column to ensure accuracy and maintain the correct proportions of the design. Additionally, it is important to double-check your work as you go along to catch any mistakes or inconsistencies before they become too difficult to correct.

In conclusion, reading needlepoint patterns is a crucial skill for any needlepoint enthusiast. By familiarizing yourself with the key, interpreting the symbols or colors, and following the instructions and directions provided, you can create stunning needlepoint designs that showcase your creativity and skill. So, grab your needle and thread, and let the art of needlepoint take you on a journey of creativity and self-expression.

The Foundation Stitches: Tent and Continental of Needlepoint: Needlepoint is a popular form of embroidery that involves stitching patterns onto a canvas using a needle and thread. One of the fundamental techniques in needlepoint is the foundation stitches, which provide the base for creating intricate designs. Two commonly used foundation stitches in needlepoint are the tent stitch and the continental stitch.

The tent stitch is a basic and versatile stitch that is often used to cover large areas of the canvas. It is worked in diagonal rows, with each stitch slanting in the same direction. The tent stitch can be worked in a variety of thread thicknesses, allowing for different levels of detail and texture in the finished piece. This stitch is ideal for creating solid blocks of color or for filling in backgrounds.

On the other hand, the continental stitch is a more complex stitch that is often used for creating fine details and outlines in needlepoint designs. It is worked in a straight line, with each stitch covering one canvas intersection. The continental stitch can be worked in a single thread or multiple threads, depending on the desired effect. This stitch is commonly used for creating intricate patterns, such as flowers, leaves, and lettering.

Both the tent stitch and the continental stitch require a basic understanding of needlepoint techniques and materials. It is important to choose the right type of canvas and thread for your project, as well as the appropriate needle size. The canvas should have a tight weave to ensure that the stitches are secure and the design is well-defined. The thread should be strong and colorfast, so that the finished piece will withstand wear and tear over time.

When working with foundation stitches in needlepoint, it is important to maintain consistent tension and stitch size throughout the project. This will ensure that the stitches are even and the design is balanced. It is also important to work from a clear and accurate pattern, as mistakes can be difficult to correct once the stitches are in place.

In conclusion, the foundation stitches of tent and continental are essential techniques in needlepoint. The tent stitch is versatile and ideal for covering large areas, while the continental stitch is more intricate and perfect for creating fine details. Both stitches require careful attention to detail and proper materials to achieve the desired result. With practice and patience, needlepoint enthusiasts can create beautiful and intricate designs using these foundation stitches.

Adding Texture with Basketweave and Diagonal Stitches of Needlepoint: Needlepoint is a popular form of embroidery that involves stitching decorative patterns onto a canvas using a needle and thread. One of the techniques used in needlepoint to add texture and visual interest to a design is the basketweave stitch. This stitch creates a woven effect that resembles a basket, hence the name.

To create the basketweave stitch, the needlepoint artist first outlines the shape or area they want to fill with the stitch. Then, they begin stitching diagonally across the canvas, weaving the thread over and under the canvas threads. This creates a series of diagonal stitches that form a woven pattern. Once the first set of diagonal stitches is complete, the artist then stitches diagonally in the opposite direction, weaving the thread over and under the previously stitched threads. This creates a crisscross pattern that further enhances the woven effect.

The basketweave stitch is often used to fill larger areas of a design, such as backgrounds or solid shapes. It adds depth and texture to the finished piece, making it more visually appealing. The woven pattern created by the stitch can also give the illusion of movement or dimension, depending on the colors and threads used.

Another technique commonly used in needlepoint to add texture is the diagonal stitch. This stitch involves stitching diagonally across the canvas, creating a series of slanted stitches. The diagonal stitch can be used in various ways to create different effects. For example, when stitched closely together, it can create a solid, textured surface. When stitched further apart, it can create a more open, lacy effect.

The diagonal stitch is often used to create patterns or motifs within a design. It can be used to outline shapes, create borders, or add detail to specific areas. The slanted stitches can also be used to create shading or gradients by using different shades of thread.

When combined with the basketweave stitch, the diagonal stitch can create even more intricate and visually stunning designs. By alternating between the two stitches, the artist can create a variety of textures and patterns within a single piece. This adds depth and dimension to the finished needlepoint, making it a true work of art.

In conclusion, adding texture to needlepoint designs using the basketweave and diagonal stitches is a popular technique among needlepoint artists. These stitches create woven and slanted patterns that add depth, dimension, and visual interest to the finished piece. Whether used individually or in combination, these stitches allow artists to create intricate and beautiful designs that showcase their skill and creativity.

Exploring Decorative Stitches of Needlepoint: Needlepoint is a popular form of embroidery that involves stitching decorative patterns onto a canvas using a needle and thread. It is a versatile and creative craft that allows individuals to express their artistic abilities and create beautiful and intricate designs. One of the most exciting aspects of needlepoint is the wide variety of decorative stitches that can be used to enhance the overall look of the piece.

When exploring decorative stitches of needlepoint, there are countless options to choose from. Each stitch has its own unique characteristics and can be used to create different effects and textures. Some stitches are simple and straightforward, while others are more complex and require a bit more skill and practice to master.

One of the most basic and commonly used stitches in needlepoint is the tent stitch. This stitch is worked in diagonal rows and creates a smooth and even surface. It is perfect for filling in large areas of a design and can be easily adapted to create different patterns and effects. The tent stitch is often used as a foundation stitch and can be combined with other stitches to add depth and dimension to a piece.

Another popular decorative stitch in needlepoint is the cross stitch. This stitch is created by making two diagonal stitches that intersect to form a small "x" shape. Cross stitches can be worked individually or in rows to create intricate patterns and designs. They are often used to create borders, lettering, and small details within a larger design.

The basketweave stitch is another commonly used stitch in needlepoint. It is a versatile stitch that creates a woven or basket-like effect. The stitch is worked in diagonal rows, alternating between vertical and horizontal stitches. The basketweave stitch is ideal for creating texture and can be used to fill in large areas or create interesting backgrounds.

Other decorative stitches in needlepoint include the French knot, the satin stitch, the long stitch, and the bullion stitch, among many others. Each stitch offers its own unique look and can be used to create different effects and textures within a design. Some stitches are more suitable for creating fine details, while others are better for filling in larger areas or adding texture to a piece.

When exploring decorative stitches of needlepoint, it is important to consider the overall design and desired effect. Experimenting with different stitches and combinations can lead to stunning and unique results. It is also helpful to consult needlepoint stitch guides and resources for inspiration and guidance on how to execute different stitches.

In conclusion, exploring the decorative stitches of needlepoint opens up a world of creative possibilities.

Creating Complex Patterns with Specialty Stitches of Needlepoint: Creating complex patterns with specialty stitches in needlepoint requires a combination of skill, creativity, and attention to detail. Needlepoint, a form of embroidery that uses a canvas and yarn, allows for the creation of intricate and beautiful designs. By incorporating specialty stitches into your needlepoint projects, you can elevate your work to a whole new level.

Specialty stitches are unique and decorative stitches that add texture, dimension, and interest to your needlepoint patterns. They can be used to create specific motifs, fill in areas, or add embellishments to your design. These stitches go beyond the basic tent stitch, which is the most commonly used stitch in needlepoint. By learning and incorporating specialty stitches into your repertoire, you can expand your creative possibilities and create stunning needlepoint pieces.

One of the key aspects of creating complex patterns with specialty stitches is understanding the different types of stitches available and how they can be combined to achieve the desired effect. There are numerous specialty stitches to choose from, including but not limited to, the French knot, the Smyrna cross, the Rhodes stitch, the Scotch stitch, and the Hungarian stitch. Each stitch has its own unique characteristics and can be used to create different textures, shapes, and patterns.

To create complex patterns, it is important to have a clear vision of the design you want to achieve. This involves planning and sketching out your pattern on graph paper or using a computer program specifically designed for needlepoint. By mapping out your design beforehand, you can determine where and how to incorporate specialty stitches to enhance the overall look of your piece.

Once you have your design planned out, it's time to start stitching. When working with specialty stitches, it is crucial to pay attention to the tension of your stitches and the placement of each stitch. This ensures that your design looks neat and professional. It may be helpful to practice the specialty stitches on a separate piece of fabric before incorporating them into your main project.

In addition to mastering the technical aspects of specialty stitches, creativity plays a significant role in creating complex patterns. Experimenting with different combinations of stitches, colors, and thread types can result in unique and visually striking designs. Don't be afraid to think outside the box and try new techniques to achieve the desired effect.

Creating complex patterns with specialty stitches in needlepoint is a labor of love that requires patience, practice, and a keen eye for detail. However, the end result is well worth the effort.

Miniature Needlepoint Projects for Quick Mastery: Miniature needlepoint projects are a great way to quickly master the art of needlepoint. These projects are small in size, making them perfect for beginners who want to practice their skills without committing to a larger, more time-consuming project. Not only do they provide a sense of accomplishment in a short amount of time, but they also allow for experimentation and creativity.

One of the advantages of miniature needlepoint projects is that they require fewer materials compared to larger projects. This means that beginners can start practicing their needlepoint skills without having to invest in a large amount of supplies. With just a small piece of fabric, a needle, and a few different colors of thread, beginners can create beautiful and intricate designs.

Another benefit of miniature needlepoint projects is that they allow beginners to focus on specific techniques and stitches. By working on a smaller scale, beginners can practice different stitches such as the basic tent stitch, the basketweave stitch, or the French knot. They can also experiment with different thread thicknesses and textures to create different effects. This focused practice helps beginners build their confidence and improve their skills more quickly.

Miniature needlepoint projects also offer the opportunity for creativity and personalization. With a smaller canvas, beginners can easily create their own designs or adapt existing patterns to suit their preferences. They can choose from a wide range of themes, such as flowers, animals, or geometric patterns, and create unique and personalized pieces of art. This creative aspect of miniature needlepoint projects adds an extra layer of enjoyment and satisfaction to the learning process.

In addition to being a great learning tool for beginners, miniature needlepoint projects also make wonderful gifts or decorative items. Once mastered, these small projects can be turned into keychains, ornaments, or framed pieces of art. They can be given as thoughtful handmade gifts or used to add a touch of charm and elegance to any space.

In conclusion, miniature needlepoint projects are an excellent choice for those looking to quickly master the art of needlepoint. They provide a sense of accomplishment in a short amount of time, require fewer materials, allow for focused practice of specific techniques, and offer the opportunity for creativity and personalization. Whether you are a beginner looking to learn a new skill or an experienced needlepointer looking for a quick and satisfying project, miniature needlepoint projects are sure to provide hours of enjoyment and a sense of achievement.

Common Mistakes and How to Fix Them of Needlepoint:

Needlepoint is a popular form of embroidery that involves stitching a design onto a canvas using a needle and thread. While it can be a relaxing and enjoyable hobby, it is not without its challenges. Many beginners make common mistakes that can affect the overall quality of their needlepoint projects. In this article, we will discuss some of these mistakes and provide tips on how to fix them.

One common mistake in needlepoint is using the wrong type of canvas. It is important to choose a canvas that is appropriate for the type of needlepoint project you are working on. For example, if you are stitching a small design with intricate details, a fine canvas with a higher thread count would be more suitable. On the other hand, if you are working on a larger project, a coarser canvas with a lower thread count may be more appropriate. Using the wrong type of canvas can result in a distorted or uneven design, so it is important to choose wisely.

Another mistake that beginners often make is using the wrong type of thread. There are many different types of thread available for needlepoint, including cotton, silk, and wool. Each type of thread has its own unique characteristics and is best suited for different types of projects. For example, cotton thread is durable and easy to work with, making it a good choice for beginners. Silk thread, on the other hand, is more delicate and is often used for more intricate designs. Using the wrong type of thread can affect the overall appearance and durability of your needlepoint project, so it is important to choose the right thread for your project.

One of the most common mistakes in needlepoint is not properly securing the thread. When stitching, it is important to make sure that the thread is securely anchored to the canvas. This can be done by making small stitches at the beginning and end of each thread, or by using a waste knot or loop start technique. Failing to secure the thread properly can result in loose stitches or the thread coming undone over time. To avoid this, take the time to properly secure your thread before starting each new section of your needlepoint project.

Another mistake that beginners often make is not properly tensioning the thread. Tensioning refers to the tightness of the stitches and is important for creating a neat and even appearance. If the thread is too loose, the stitches will be uneven and the design may appear distorted.

Tips for Tension and Consistency of Needlepoint: Needlepoint is a popular form of embroidery that involves stitching a design onto a canvas using a needle and thread. One of the key aspects of creating a beautiful needlepoint piece is achieving the right tension and consistency in your stitches. This not only ensures that the design looks neat and professional, but also helps to prevent any puckering or distortion of the canvas.

Here are some tips to help you achieve the perfect tension and consistency in your needlepoint:

1. Choose the right canvas: The type of canvas you use can greatly affect the tension and consistency of your stitches. It's important to select a canvas that is sturdy and has a tight weave. This will provide a solid foundation for your stitches and help to maintain their shape.

2. Use the right thread: The type of thread you use can also impact the tension and consistency of your stitches. It's important to choose a

thread that is appropriate for the canvas and design you are working on. Thicker threads may require looser tension, while thinner threads may require tighter tension. Experiment with different threads to find the one that works best for your project.

3. Start with a taut frame: Before you begin stitching, make sure your canvas is stretched tightly on a frame or hoop. This will help to maintain consistent tension throughout your work and prevent any sagging or distortion of the canvas.

4. Practice proper stitching technique: The way you stitch can also affect the tension and consistency of your needlepoint. Make sure to insert your needle straight into the canvas and pull the thread through smoothly. Avoid pulling too tightly or leaving too much slack in your stitches. Practice your stitching technique to ensure that your stitches are even and consistent.

5. Check your tension regularly: As you work on your needlepoint project, it's important to regularly check the tension of your stitches. This can be done by gently tugging on the canvas to see if it feels too loose or too tight. Adjust your tension as needed to maintain a consistent and even appearance.

6. Block your finished piece: Once you have completed your needlepoint project, it's a good idea to block it to ensure that the tension and consistency of your stitches are maintained. Blocking involves wetting the canvas and then stretching it back into shape. This can help to even out any uneven stitches and give your piece a polished and professional look.

By following these tips, you can achieve the perfect tension and consistency in your needlepoint projects.

Making the Most of Needlepoint: Needlepoint is a versatile and enjoyable craft that allows individuals to create beautiful and intricate designs using a needle and thread. Whether you are a beginner or an experienced needlepointer, there are several ways to make the most of this creative and relaxing activity.

First and foremost, it is important to choose the right materials for your needlepoint project. The type of fabric, thread, and needle you use can greatly impact the final result. When selecting fabric, consider the weave and texture to ensure it is suitable for your desired design. Additionally, choose high-quality threads that are durable and colorfast to ensure your needlepoint creation will stand the test of time. Lastly, select the appropriate needle size for your fabric and thread to ensure smooth and even stitching.

Once you have gathered your materials, it is time to plan your design. Take the time to sketch out your desired pattern or use a pre-made needlepoint pattern. Consider the colors, shapes, and overall composition of your design to create a visually appealing and balanced piece. If you are new to needlepoint, starting with a simpler design can help build your skills and confidence before tackling more complex projects.

When it comes to stitching, there are several techniques to consider. The most common stitch used in needlepoint is the tent stitch, which is a diagonal stitch that creates a smooth and even surface. However, there are many other stitches to explore, such as the basketweave stitch, the cross stitch, and the French knot. Experimenting with different stitches can add texture and dimension to your needlepoint project.

In addition to the actual stitching, there are several ways to enhance your needlepoint creation. Consider adding embellishments such as beads, sequins, or ribbons to add a touch of sparkle and interest. You can also incorporate different textures by using different types of threads, such as metallic or silk threads. Additionally, framing your finished needlepoint piece or turning it into a functional item, such as a pillow or a tote bag, can further showcase your creativity and make your needlepoint project more versatile.

Finally, don't forget to take care of your needlepoint creations. Proper storage and cleaning can help preserve the beauty and longevity of your finished pieces. Store your needlepoint in a cool, dry place to prevent damage from moisture or pests. If your needlepoint becomes dirty, gently spot clean it with a mild detergent and cold water, taking care not to rub or scrub the stitches.

INTRODUCTION TO NEEDLEPOINT

Needlepoint is a kind of canvas work, a type of counted thread embroidery in which yarn is stitched through a stiff open weave canvas. Traditionally needlepoint designs totally cover the canvas. Although needlepoint may be done in a variety of stitches, many needlepoint patterns use only a simple tent stitch and depend on color changes in the yarn to construct the pattern. Needlepoint is the oldest form of canvas work.

The level of detail in needlepoint depends on the thread count of the fundamental mesh fabric. Due to the intrinsic lack of suppleness of needlepoint, ordinary uses include eyeglass cases, holiday ornaments, pillows, purses, upholstery, and wall hangings.

CHAPTER ONE

STORAGE BIN

CHAPTER ONE
STORAGE BIN

Assuming you have a lot of stuff, and you need a specially sized, exclusively crafted way to store them, looks no farther than plastic canvas. Here, I'll teach you the best way to create a basic lidded box, and give it your own unique style.

MATERIALS

2 sheets 10-count plastic canvas

Sharpie marker

Pair of Scissors

Tapestry needle

Yarn or other material that can work well

Fabric scraps

Hand-sewing needle and thread

Working surface

DIRECTIONS
SIZING THE BOX

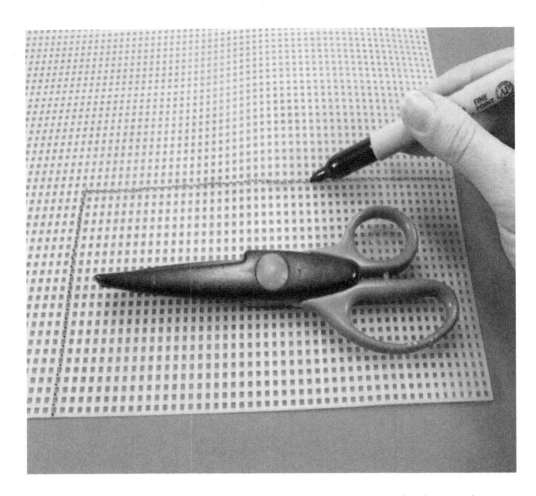

STAGE 1: Get the items you need to store, and place them on the plastic canvas, close to a corner. Then, at that point, male use of a Sharpie to stamp the base board of the box. I love to make my boxes somewhat bigger than I need, so they'll have space for future stuff.

Cut this piece of the canvas.

STAGE 2: Next, sort out how deep your box should be to fit the things you need to store. You can estimate this with a ruler, or eyeball it.

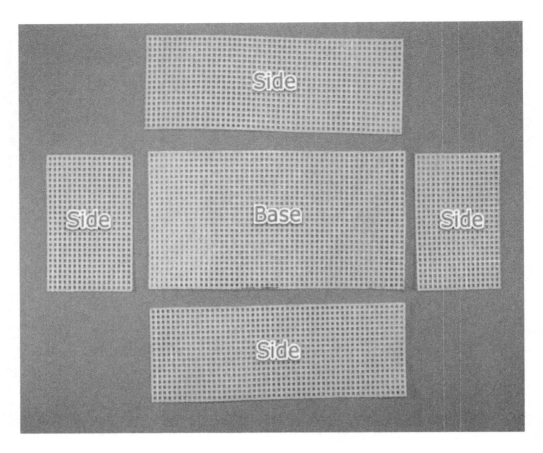

STAGE 3: Using the base you cut in stage 1 as an estimating guide, cut out 4 sides for your box. Make these side boards as tall as the estimation you chose in stage 2.

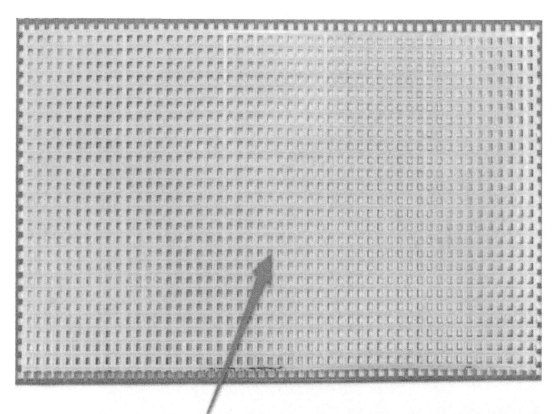

Base piece

STAGE 4: Now, to make the top for you're the box, you'll need to cut a piece that is slightly bigger than the bottom. Make use of your base piece as an estimating guide, and cut the lid piece so it's 1 row of squares bigger on every one of the 4 sides, as displayed above. (I do this, coincidentally, so the completed cover will fit pleasantly on the completed box.)

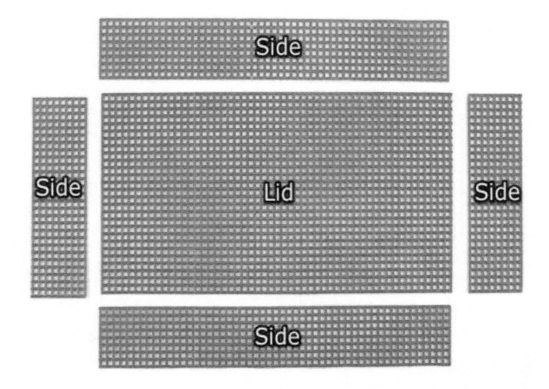

STAGE 5: Then, make use of the lid piece as a gauging manual to cut 4 sides for the lid. They ought to be between 1"–2" deep. You should now have 10 cut bits of plastic canvas.

STITCHING THE BOX

A few crafters don't care for plastic material work since they think: a) it must be covered with traditional needlepoint, and) all that needlepoint is too tedious.

But on a serious note, there's a world of fascinating needlepoint stitches that work up considerably more rapidly than the traditional continental stitch.

Also, you can "consider new ideas," figuratively speaking, with regards to picking your stitchery materials. You can make use of any worsted-weight cotton or fleece yarn, obviously, but as you can see here, paper raffia (accessible at craft stores) and thin ribbon likewise make intriguing impacts.

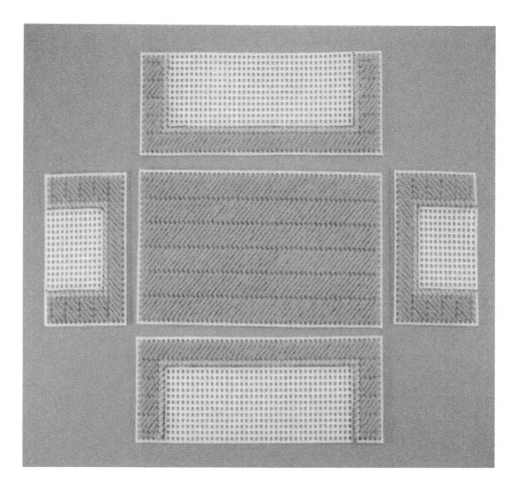

For this box, I'm stitching with cotton yarn. I'm utilizing the Slanted Gobelin Stitch since it makes lots of progress rapidly. And afterward, to make things much quicker, I will add some fabrics supplements to cover portions of the canvas. In this picture, you can see the base and side bits of my box, all stitched and prepared for fabric.

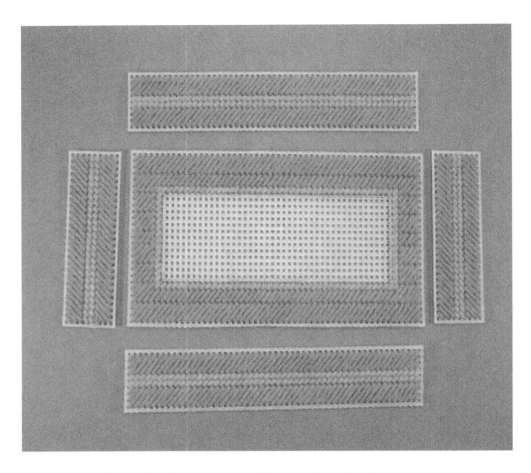

Here you have the lid pieces, additionally stitched and prepared for a fabric insert.

ADDING FABRIC

STAGE 6: This project is an incredible method to make use of little scraps of a most loved fabric. Just cut a piece that is around 1/2" bigger on all sides than the uncovered side of the canvas.

Then, at that point fold under each of the 4 sides of the fabric so the piece fits pleasantly into this opening. Press the folds.

STAGE 7: Thread a hand-sewing needle. Put the fabric over the plastic canvas, arranging it according to the uncovered area. Then, bring the needle up through one of the openings in the canvas, getting the edge of the fabric as displayed here.

Then, pass the needle down through the same opening. Move to the following hole and repeat this stitch, and the following, etc till you've stitched each of the 4 edges of the fabric down.

GATHERING THE BOX

I'm going to stitch every one of the pieces together now, so it's a good time to discuss how to begin and end a strand of yarn.

To combine 2 pieces, place the wrong sides together, lining every one of the holes. Then, at that point, pass the needle through 1 layer of canvas only, getting the yarn through till you have about a 2" tail sitting between the 2 pieces.

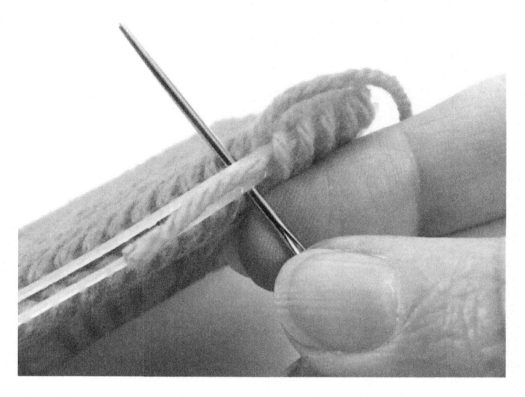

Get the pieces together with a whipstitch, getting that remaining loose end in the first stitch as displayed. A whipstitch, incidentally, simply involves passing your needle through the two pieces of material the same way.

Toward the end of the seam, you can tie off a strand of yarn by passing it beneath certain stitches at the back of the canvas, as displayed here, and afterward cutting it.

STAGE 8: begin the assembly procedure by joining each of the 4 sides of the box to the base piece.

STAGE 9: Thereafter, fold the sides up and whipstitch them together at each corner. Stitch from the base to the top — it's a lot simpler to tie off the strands toward the end of each seam that way.

STAGE 10: finally, whip stitch around the top edge of the box to complete it. At the point when you're stitching around the edges of the box. Take a few more stitches — this will assist cover up the canvas at those points.

STAGE 11: Repeat stages 15-17 to gather a lid for your box, and you're through!

CHAPTER TWO
MOD TABLE RUNER

The majority of big-box craft stores possess these interesting PC circles, and they're helpful for lots of projects. I love this table runner for its free-formless. You should simply stitch up a lot of circles, and afterward put them in any configuration you like – you can make a more circular arrangement for a round table. You could make a more drawn out and more slender one for a credenza.

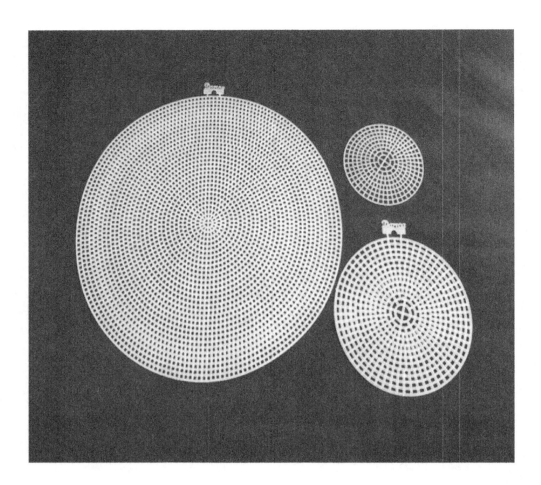

These are the generally accessible circles sizes: 6", 4.5", and 3". You might see that my table linen runner seems to possess lots more bigger sizes than these in it – that is on the grounds that I cut some of my circles down a bit to make more variety. (Everything you do is removed the external rows until you're satisfied with the size.) I make use of 21 circles in my table runner; you may require more or less than that.

STITCHING THE CIRCLES

I stitched the circles with good o1' tent stitch.

You could truly make use of any decorative needlepoint stitch here, as long it'll adjust to the circular pattern of the holes in the canvas.

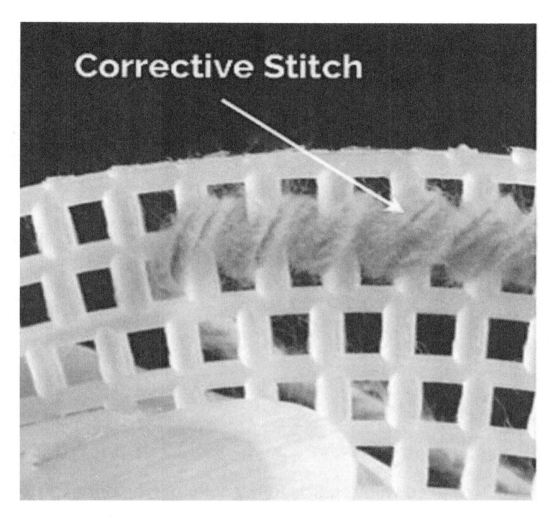

There's one significant stitch to notice when you're tent-stitching PC circles. Depending upon their size, these circles will have spots where the holes don't line impeccably, or where they're a bit bigger than normal. That will at times make your stitches get excessively long and excessively horizontal as you work your direction around.

When this occurs, just accept what I call a "corrective stitch." That's the spot where you begin your stitch in another hole; however you end it in the same hole as the past stitch. That corrects the point, and your stitching will look more ordinary going forward. You'll have to create more corrective stitches in your rows as you draw nearer to the middle of most circles.

I was pretty relaxed with regards to my color placement as I stitched my circles. I picked six colors of my favorite Sugar 'n Cream. I began at the external row of each round and stitched toward the middle, changing colors when I felt like it.

Thereafter, I edged every one of the circles with overcast stitch. A few circles need two stitches in each hole to get great coverage, and others need just one stitch for every hole. It all depends on the size of the circle and where you may have trimmed it.

After each one of the circles have been stitched and edged, it's an ideal opportunity to back them. I just traced each circle onto some felt with a fine-point marker, and afterward cut them out right inside my tracing line. I then, gum the felt circles to the backs of the PC ones, and set them under some heavy books to dry.

(Expert tip: PC has enormous openings that permit glue to ooze through. Put some wax paper on the two sides of your circles to protect your books and your work surface).

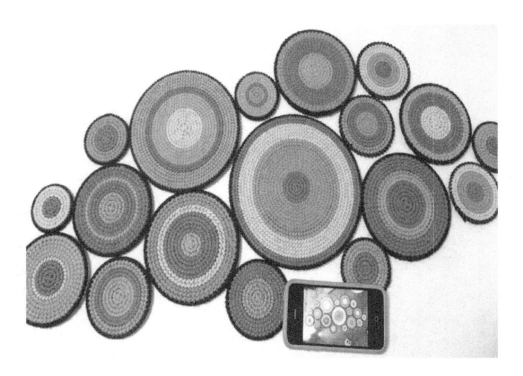

Immediately, I spread my completed circles out on a table and moved them around till I had a design I loved. I highly suggest snapping a picture of that layout – you'll require that to refer back to again and again as you join these little puppies. (Truly, don't skip this process. I usually think I'll simply remember how placed them, and I never ever do.)

JOINING THE CIRCLES

The next stage is to join those circles together. It's the simplest to do this with your circles all spread out before you, and that photograph you took before not far off.

Prior to starting the process, I'll disclose to you that the entire secret to a decent, flat table runner is SMALL POINT OF CONTACT. It's enticing, when you're stitching these things together, to stitch along a wide region so the two circles are absolutely stable against one another. That is an error! You need your stitched circles to be able to "roll" a little to this side or that side - that way, as you continue to add new circles, you'll have the option to tenderly adjust every one of their positions so they fit together perfectly.

When you have every one of the circles stitched, trust me – the entire thing will be good and stable.

I suggest making use of a solid, fairly thick thread for joining your circles. Upholstery threads or quilting threads are acceptable choices. You can likewise work with a double strand of standard sewing thread, however with doubled thresd, there's consistently a possibility that it'll get tangled as you stitch.

I'll demo the join utilizing a contrasting color of string, yet you'll need to make use of one that matches your edging.

Begin joining with one of your bigger circles that is close to the middle of your design. Thread up a sewing needle with around 12" of thread, and tie a nice large knot eventually. Pass your needle through certain stitches at the back of your first circle – everything we're doing here is catching that knot in the yarn to anchor it. Draw the needle and thread entirely through.

Set the circle down once more, placing it in its area in your layout. Turn this circle so the thread is coming out right where this circle will connect with the one close to it.

Then, pass your needle down through the edge of that adjacent circle as displayed. (It's ideal to do this pass with the two circles laying flat on the table.)

Repeat this procedure once again to get two stitches between the two circles. Presently it's ideal to get them and grasp them in your hands. Stitch them together a few more times, drawing the thread fairly tight. Simply make each join point is close to 2-3 holes wide – you can make a few stitches in each of those holes for strength, however keep that join point small!

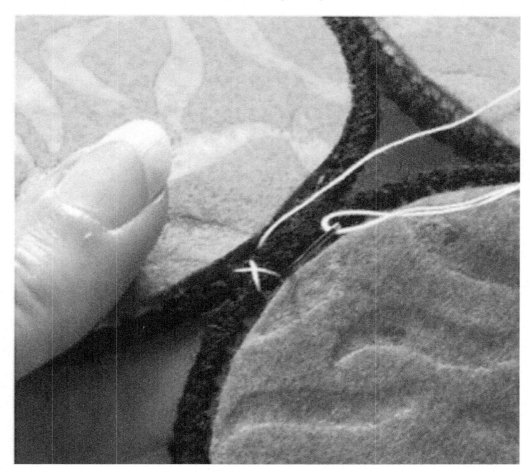

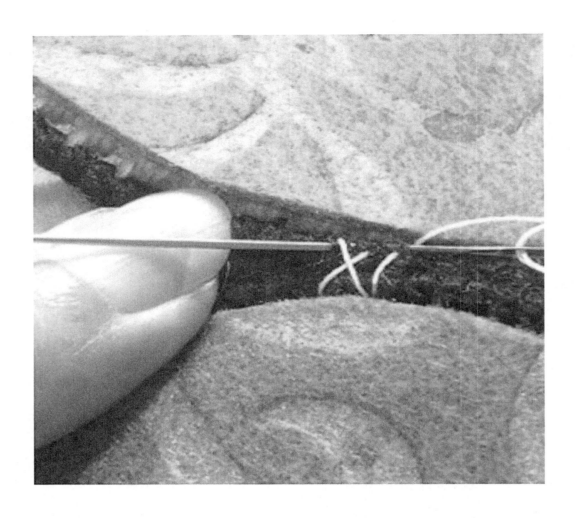

Immediately you are through with those stitches, it's an ideal opportunity to create a good, strong knot at the back. Pass your needle under a few stitches and get the thread through till you have a little loop. Thereafter, pass your needle through that loop about two times. Drag the thread tight, and you have a knot. Cut your thread and continue on to the next join point.

I suggest checking the alignment of all your assembled circles often against your photograph as you work on this part of the project. Place your table runner back out flat on your table before you join each new circle.

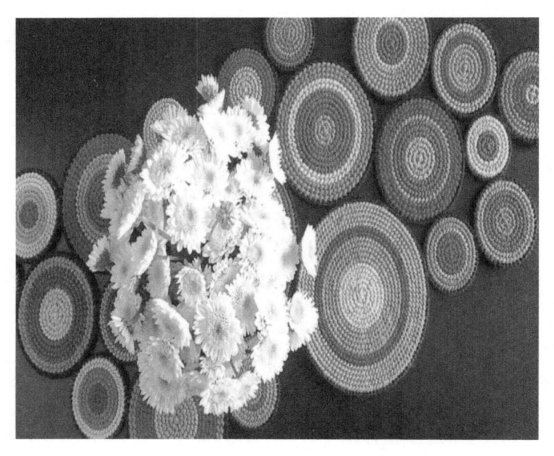

After you've joined each of your circles, you're through! You may get the completed table runner in your hands and check whether there are any points where the join between two circles feels a bit floppy. You should return and do some more stitching at those focuses, just to be extra amazing with regards to things.

I feel this design would also be pretty delivered in neutral colors, or as neutrals with little pops of colors in the middle, or even as a monochromatic sort of thing. What varieties will you come up with?

CHAPTER THREE

NEEDLEPOINT STITCH MARKER CASE

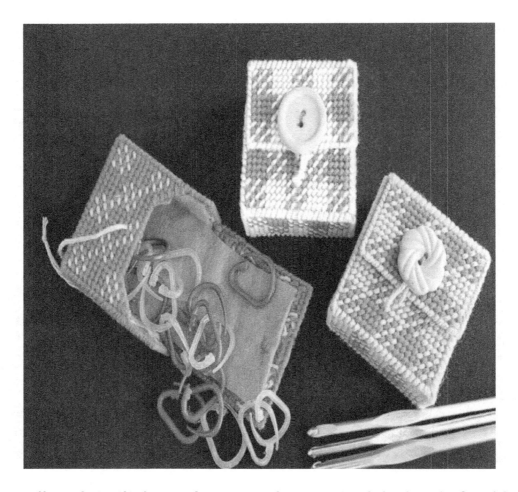

This needlepoint stitch marker case is a cottonish dandy for 10 count plastic canvas. It makes ideal coverage with a single strand, regardless of whether you're utilizing short stitches or long ones. It's also fundamentally less expensive than stitching with embroidery floss or pearl cotton. What's more, the color range is truly beautiful.

MATERIALS

Cottonish yarn (chose whatever color you desire)

Canvas

Tapestry needle

Pair of scissors

Felt

Non permanent marker

Super glue

Buttons

So this convenient case is to keep your stitch markers in, so they aren't spread all around the bottom of your knitting/stitch bag. These little cases make up very fast, and they're an ideal method to go through the Cotton-ish you have left over from different projects.

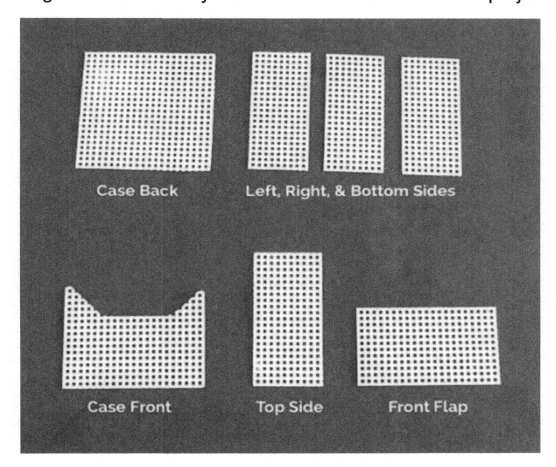

To start with, you'll cut some 10-count canvas. You'll need exact counting here so the stitching pattern fits, so measure your canvas by checking the holes. Here are the pieces you'll require:

Case Back: 21 holes x 21 openings, cut 1

Left, Right, and Base Sides: 21 holes x 9 holes, cut 3

Top Side: 21 holes x 10 openings, cut 1

Case Front: 21 holes x 16 holes, with a small piece cut out of the top edge (Just eyeguage that; it's an opening to aid you reach in and get your markers.)

Front Flap: 21 holes x 12 holes

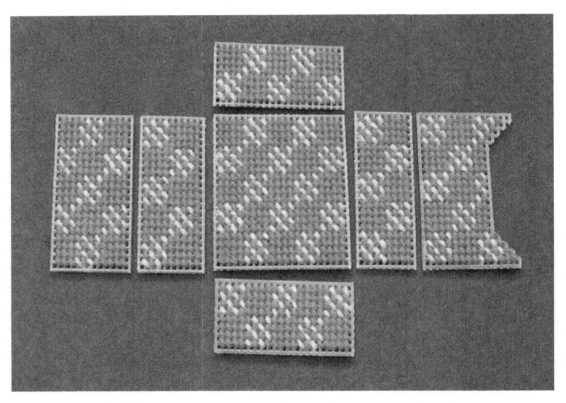

Thereafter, stitch every one of the pieces. Presently, I know patterns are useful for certain sorts of projects, but this is one where I think you can be considerably more relaxed with regards to it.

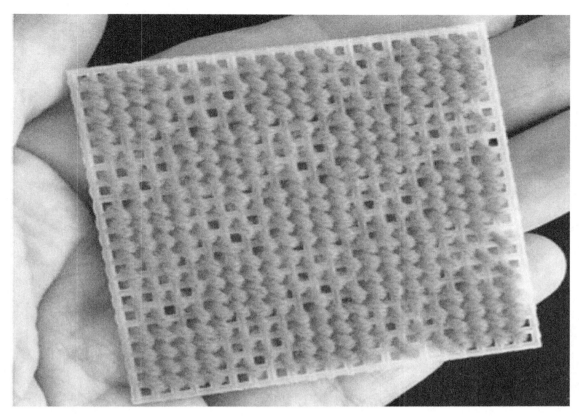

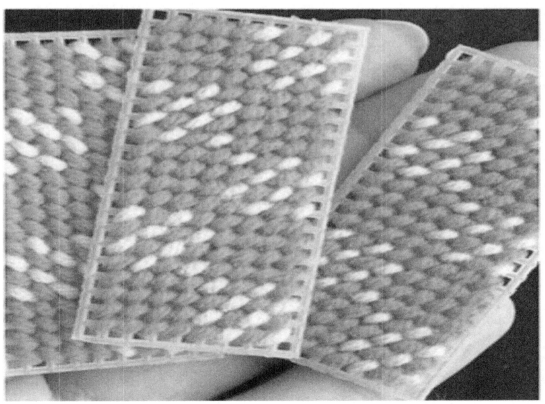

To create a checkered pattern, here's everything you ought to do. I began at the base right corner of each piece. I stitched a square made of four stitches across and four up. Then, over that, I created another square where each row has two stitches, and they substitute position.

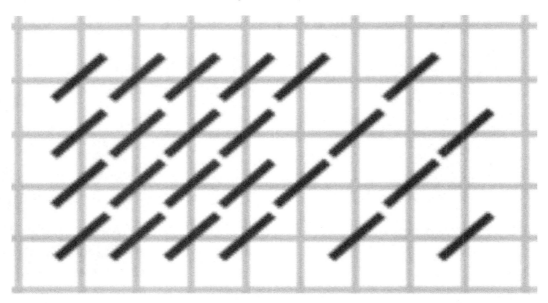

This unit is the structure block for the entire pattern. I filled each piece with that, working in vertical rows from base to top, and afterward I filled in the empty regions with a second color.

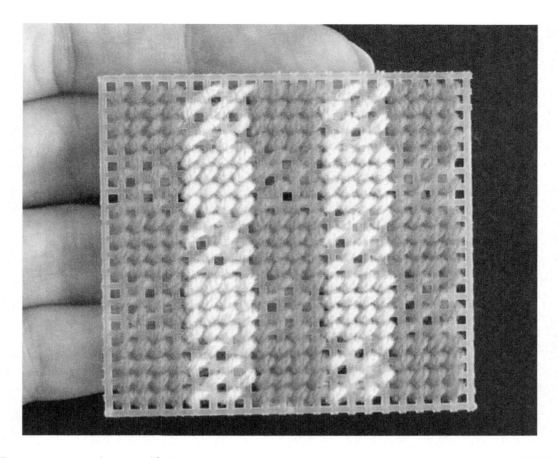

To create a beautiful checker pattern, I did likewise correct thing, however changed color each row. Then, I filled in with the contrary color. (You can see this pattern in action on two of my completed examples at the top of the post.)

But you can truly use any stitch pattern you prefer here – my little checkered dealio is only one of unlimited options. Search for needlepoint stitches, or stitch a pattern of stripes, or a solid color from the web. Try not to make it too confounded, simply have fun with it!

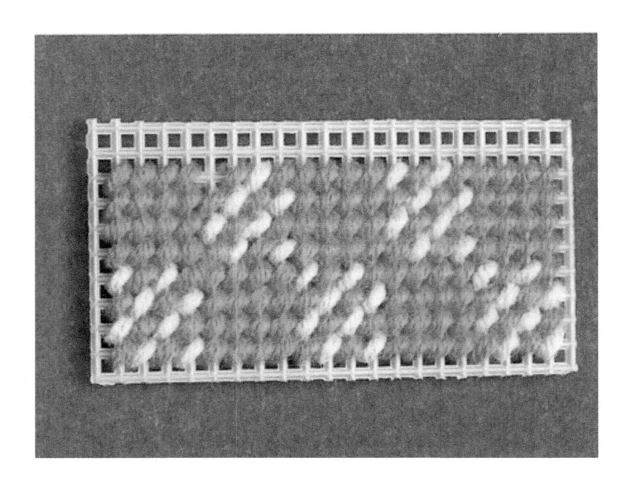

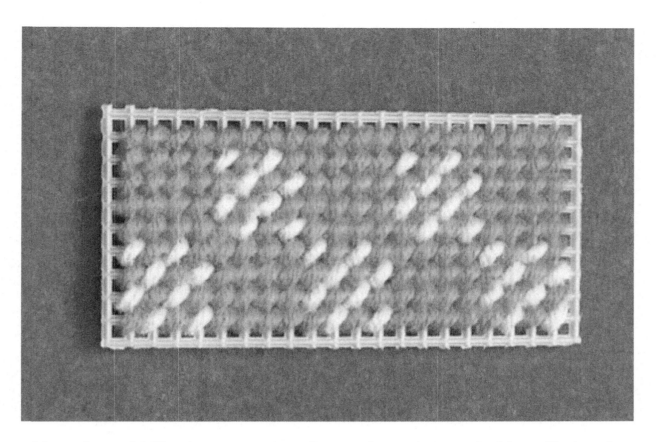

Now, I would like to create two fast points about stitching. To begin with, notice that the top side of the case is one row of squares wider than the other three sides. This additional width permits the cover fold to fit appropriately over the front of the case. So in case you're using my checkered pattern, you'll need to add one additional row of stitches to this piece, as you see here.

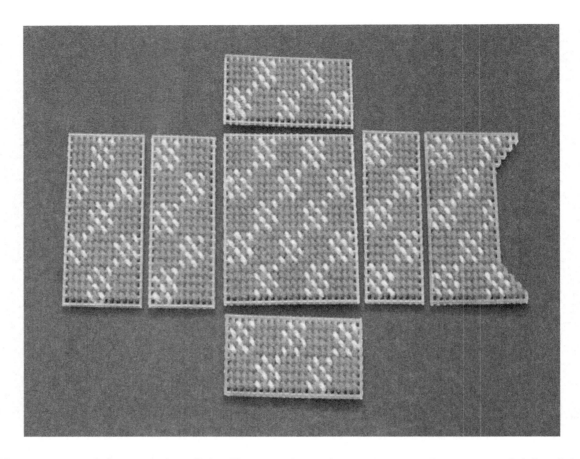

The second fast point (kindly pardon the repeat photograph) is this: in case you're making use of a checkered pattern, I suggest stitching the back piece first and afterward using that to dictate how you position the basic pattern unit on all the other pieces. However, if you mess up a bit, as I did with the top side of my case here, don't be too hard on yourself. The general impression will be a checkered example, I guarantee!

Great! We'll gather this together now! Sew the top, left, right, and base sides to the back of the case. It's ideal if you can begin with a beautiful long strand of yarn, so you can do this in a single seam. I'm utilizing a whip stitch here.

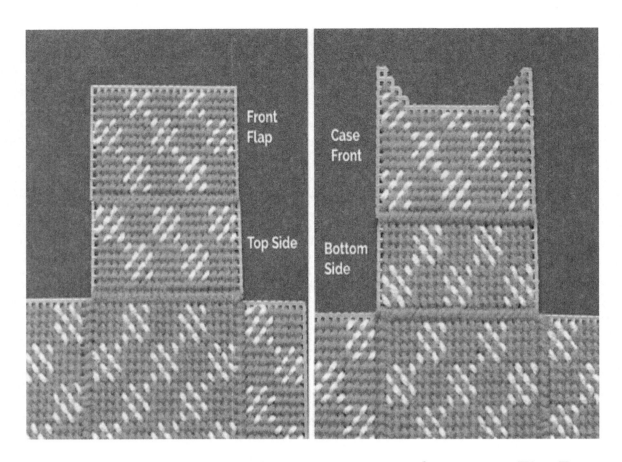

Then, you'll stitch the remaining two pieces of the case. The Front Flap piece is joined to the Top Side. The Case Front piece is joined to the Bottom Side. (Keep in mind, the way in which you differentiate them is that the Top Side has that extra row of stitches.)

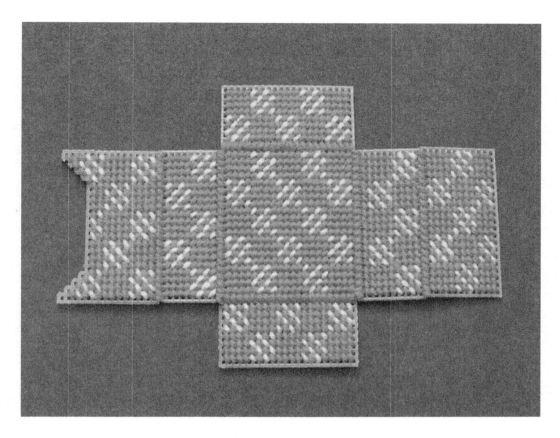

So, the entire thing appears as though this when you're done.

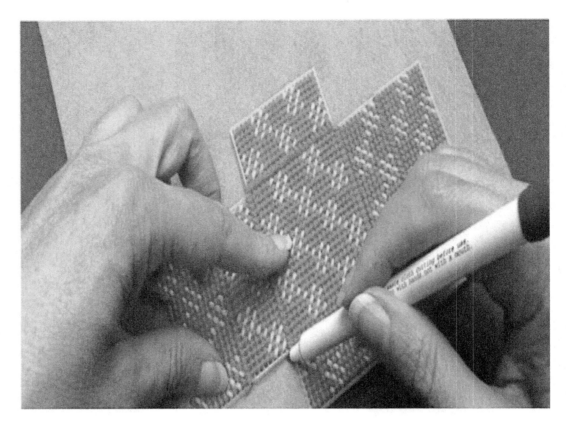

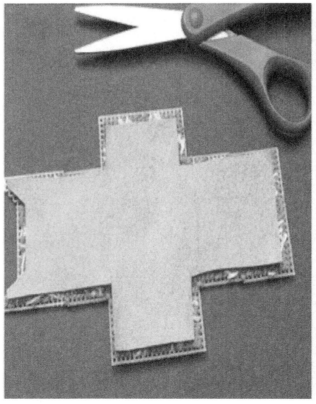
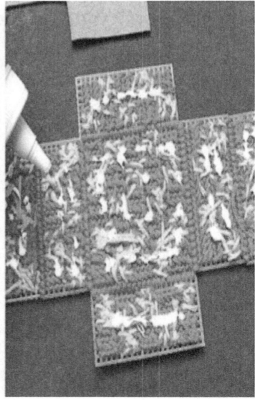

Assuming you need to, you can give your case a relaxed liner, similar to this. To start with, trace the flat case onto a piece of felt. Then, cut inside your tracing lines by a decent 1/8". You need the felt to be smaller than the case on all sides as you see above, so continue to trimming the felt until it fits.

Then, lightly gum it to the back of the case piece. Try not to put any glue on the joints where you stitched two pieces together! If you do, you end up making your case too stiff to use.

 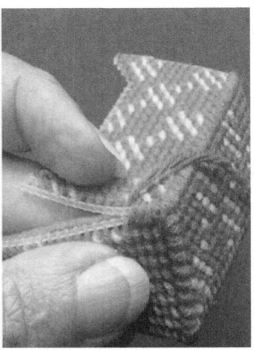

Presently, we'll start sewing up the sides of the case, starting here at the front piece. Bring your needle up at the point you see above. Then, seam the base side in to meet the case front, and stitch those edges together.

Immediately you arrive at the corner, take an additional stitch in that last hole and afterward round the corner so you can begin stitching the next edge. Take two stitches in the first hole and afterward keep stitching until you arrive at the end of the case front.

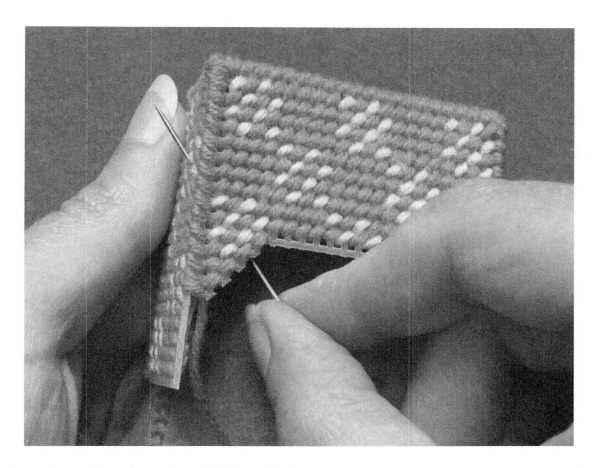

The most ideal way to finish off these seams is to pass your needle through some stitches at the back of the case, beneath that felt liner, and afterward bring the needle out somewhere on the case, as you see above. Then, get the yarn through and clip it flush with the side of the case.

Repeat this procedure to sew up the opposite side of the case.

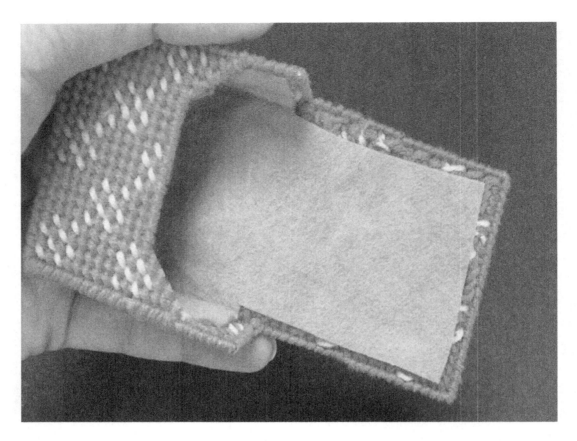

In conclusion, use overcast stitch to complete the whole remaining edge, which runs along the front of the case and around the top side and front flap. Finish this stitch the same way as I portrayed above.

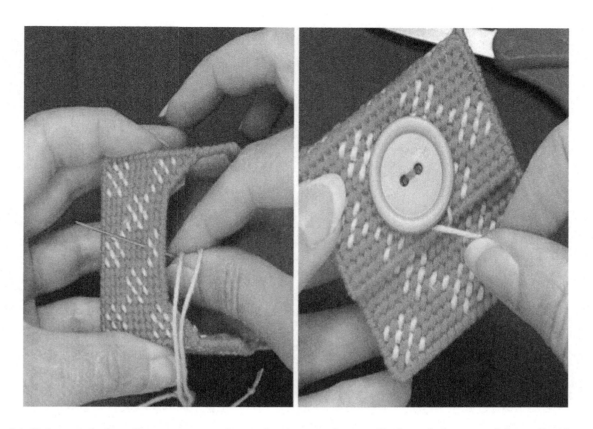

At this point, all you need to do is make a little closure. Here's the way I do that: first, I thread about a 6" strand of yarn onto a needle, and tie a large knot at the end. Then, I pass the needle out through the front of the case, so the yarn comes through directly beneath where the front flap overlaps it. Get the thread through.

Then, sew an enormous and beautiful button to that front flap. You can wrap the strand of yarn over the button a few times to make a decent, secure closure. I normally cut back any excess yarn and tie a little knot in the opposite end so it can't slip back through the case wall.

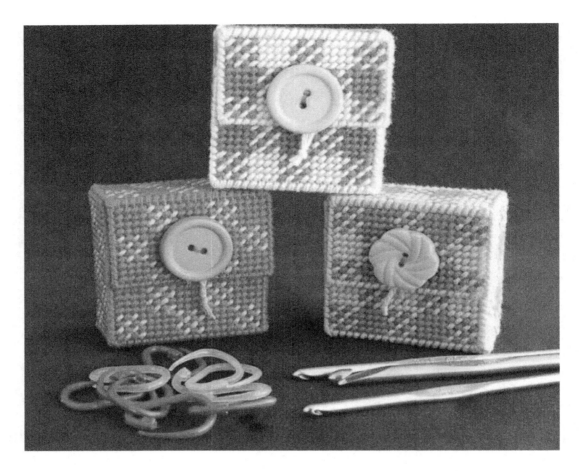

… And you're doe! Fill it with your join markers of choice and appreciate.

CHAPTER FOUR

LAZY DAISY EMBROIDERY

Lazy daisy stitch possesses the right tone to its name to prepare you for some good embroidery. This stitch is very simple and an easy variation of the chain stitch. The Lazy Daisy is also called detached chain stitch, so if you can know chain stitch, then Lazy Daisy is just an shortened form of this.

The lazy daisy stitch is a nice 'garden' stitch ideal for leaves and flowers, so if you cherish gardens and greenery, sit back and try this extremely calm, but creative embroidery stitch. The flowers might be huge or little and can have varying numbers of petals.

SUPPLIES

Hoop - The lazy daisy stitch just like other needlework is most excellent done on a hoop to hold the cloth tight and to reduce wrinkles and pulling in your flowers.

Thread - Use a sturdy thread that doesn't split. I make use of embroidery floss with all the six strands. At this thickness, I utilized a single-threaded needle (thread not doubled over) (thread not doubled over).

Needles – make use of an embroidery thread appropriate for the fabric you are using. If you have any difficulty threading the thick thread, use a needle threader to make your work much easier.

STAGE 1 - ENTER THE NET.

Take the needle to the base of one of the petals from below (1). The flower center can be as large or as tiny as you want. I got a center quite open.

If you wish to have a little center, draw the needle closer.

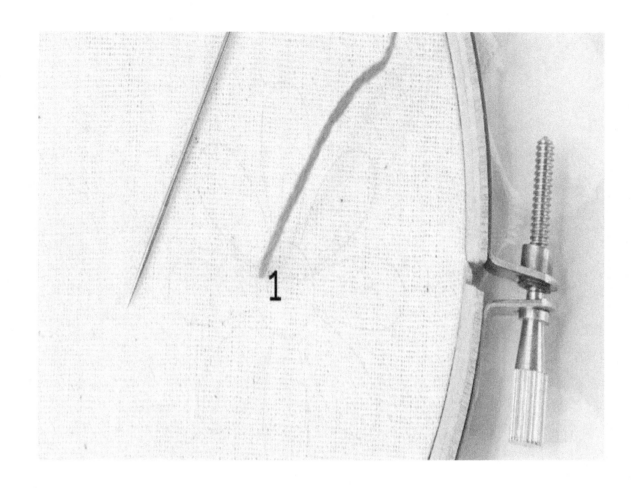

STAGE 2 – BASE

Place the needle close to (1) at the bottom of the other side of the petal at (2).

The distance between (1) and should be small (2).

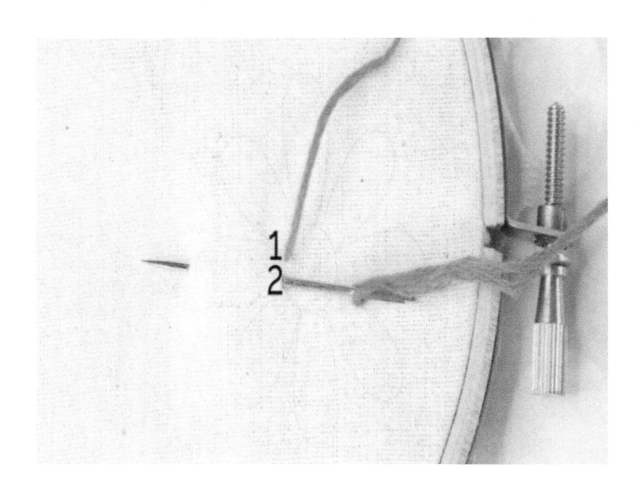

STAGE 3 - PETAL FIRST

Take out the petal's tip with the needle at 3.

Notice: wrap the thread below the needle tip.

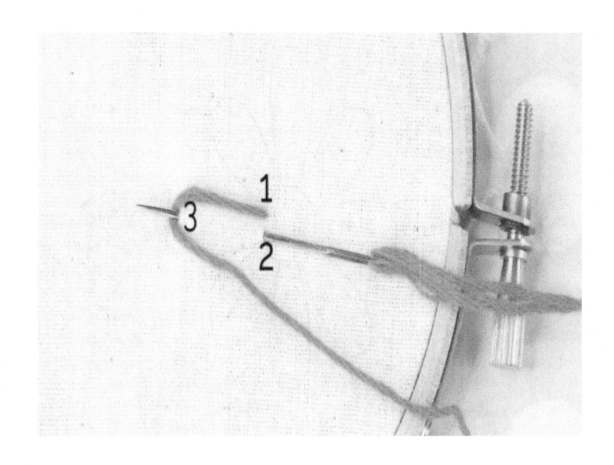

STAGE 4 - SECURE PETAL

At 4, place the needle on the other side of the loop and at 5, the base of a new petal should come up.

The thread which passes between (3) and (4) holds down the tip of your petal loop.

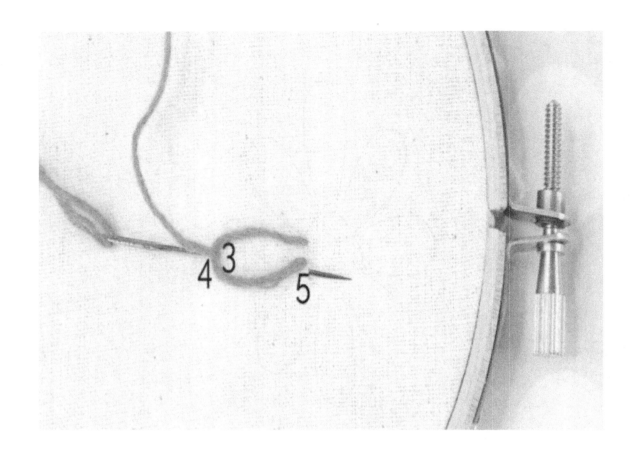

STAGE 5 – REPEAT

Repeat now as you pass through the flower. You can see that I can add a few knots for a color pop because my center is fairly large. You may make it very modest and unnoticeable in your centre. This flower is also very huge, so details may be easily seen. Petals and the center mix much more for smaller flowers. There is no correct or wrong personal preference, just like most sewing.

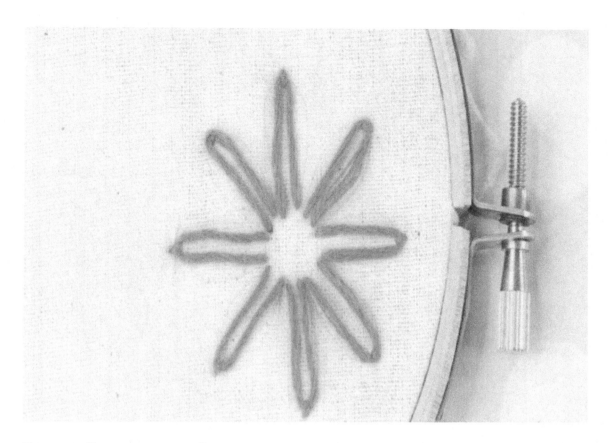

Depending on your flower design, every individual chain or Lazy Daisy begins separately.

These small flowers look lovely with some contrasting French knots in the center. Also with a backstitch or stem stitch, some stems can be added.

LAZY DAISY STITCH TIPS

Round Petals - Do not tighten long threads lest you will close your petal. Make petals beautifully round by letting loops loose. In my picture of hot pink you can see above, that the stitches that fasten petals at the end are more obvious when you tighten them. This isn't always good or bad, but only personal preference.

Thread Quality — Use broken floss or thread that is not divided when the petals begin to look chaotic like my blue one below.

LAZY DAISY STITCH – THE INCLUSION

The Lazy Daisy's stitch is really simple. You can make all kinds of flower petals long and short, full or widely spread using the chain stitch pattern. It's a beautiful basic stitch which looks amazing in a embroidered garden.

CHAPTER FIVE

TINY HEARTS WITH SCROLL STITCH

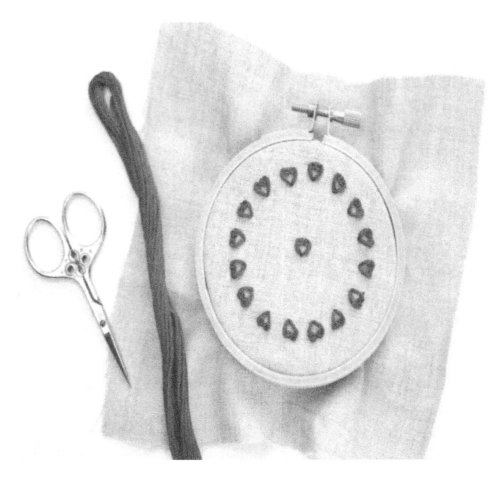

Embroidery little design is entertaining, but may be difficult as well. Sometimes it is advisable to use a different stitch than you would assume to be the way to make something extra small. Two fly-stitches, stitched as scallops are one technique to browse small hearts, but this specific heart employs scroll-stitch.

TIP

Scroll stitch is often stitched between left and right and left. But to build a heart, working vertically is helpful.

TOOLS / MATERIALS

Embroidery needle

Embroidery floss

GUIDELINES

STITCH THE HEART'S LEFT SIDE.

Put the needle through the fabric and produce from left to right a small horizontal stitch. The point of the needle should be a little below 1/4 inch above where the thread is filled with the fabric. It can help to turn your hoop clockwise 90 degrees when you stitch.

Wrap the floss below the needle's left side, then under the stitch and on the right hand side. Pull the needle and it will emerge in the first half of the heart.

TIP

The needle should point to the center when stitching each half of the heart and the loop of the thread should appear a little like half a heart before you draw the needle through it. The stitch was probably not done properly if the stitch does not seem to have a tiny scroll shape and should be removed and stitched again.

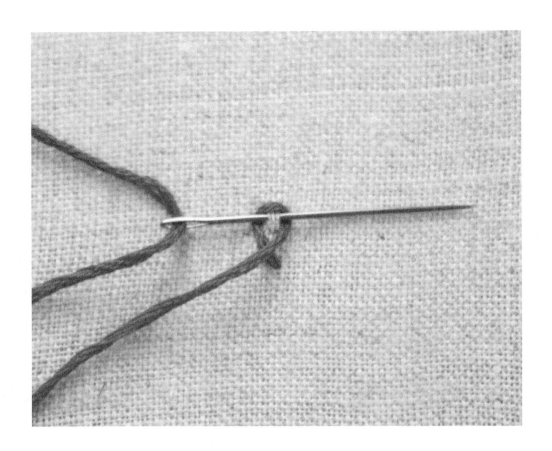

TACK THE STITCH IN PLACE

Take down the needle right up and through the fabric to the right of the thread. Don't pull it too tight, or you might pull the stitch.

STITCH THE HEART'S RIGHT SIDE

Forming a second scroll point on the right half of the heart worked the other way around. Take a horizontal stitch from right to left at the bottom of the heart. The stitch should be parallel to the first stitch that is lower than the heart top. It can assist to rotate your hoop 90 degrees in the opposite direction while you stitch.

Wrap the thread below the needle's right side, over the stitch, and under the needle's left side. Pull the needle and tackle the scroll down like the first half.

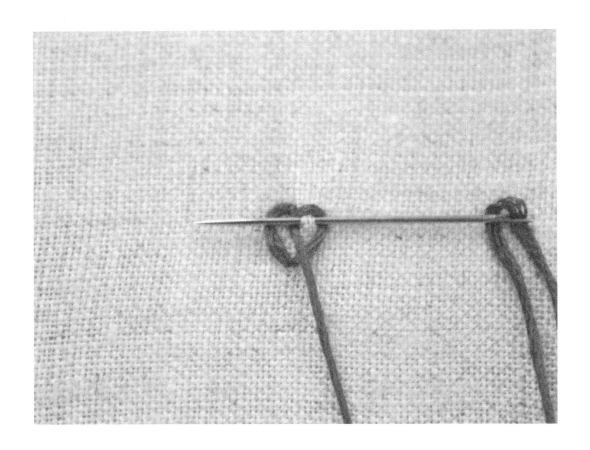

COMPLETE THE TINY HEART

It should look like the photo below in your completed heart. The heart halves can raise from the fabric and this all right—they're three-dimensional. You can also flatten them a little by pressing them with your finger.

Trace two circles using a water-soluble pen in order to construct the ring of hearts. One circle should be approximately 1/4 inch wider. Use the traced circles as a reference for the top and the base of your stitches to add hearts around the ring.

These hearts would also perfectly fill a silhouette of the heart.

Learning to construct little tiny hearts can do some work, but they're so sweet and adaptable you're happy to do it.

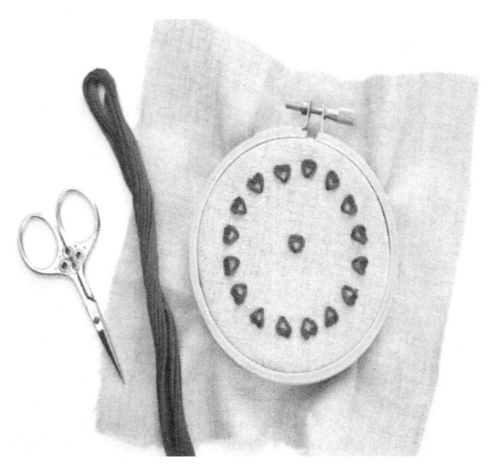

Your tiny embroidered hearts is ready!

Printed in Great Britain
by Amazon